Published by
Balaji

Title: COOKIES

Purchase our books online from:

AMAZON

THE AUTHOR
Ji saays

CONTENT

Sugar Cookies

Ingredients

3 cups all-purpose flour
3/4 teaspoon baking powder
1/4 teaspoon salt
1 cup unsalted butter, softened
1 cup sugar
1 egg, beaten
1 tablespoon milk
Powdered sugar, for rolling out dough

Directions

Sift together flour, baking powder, and salt. Set aside. Place butter and sugar in large bowl of electric stand mixer and beat until light in color. Add egg and milk and beat to combine. Put mixer on low speed, gradually add flour, and beat until mixture pulls away from the side of the bowl. Divide the dough in half, wrap in waxed paper, and refrigerate for 2 hours.
Preheat oven to 375 degrees F.
Sprinkle surface where you will roll out dough with powdered sugar. Remove 1 wrapped pack of dough from refrigerator at a time, sprinkle rolling pin with powdered sugar, and roll out dough to 1/4-inch thick. Move the dough around and check underneath frequently to make sure it is not sticking. If dough has warmed during rolling, place cold cookie sheet on top for 10 minutes to chill. Cut into desired shape, place at least 1-inch apart on greased baking sheet, parchment, or silicone baking mat, and bake for 7 to 9 minutes or until cookies are just beginning to turn brown around the edges, rotating cookie sheet halfway through baking time. Let sit on baking sheet for 2 minutes after removal from oven and then move to complete cooling on wire rack. Serve as is or ice as desired. Store in airtight container for up to 1 week.

Shortbread Cookies

Ingredients

3/4 pound unsalted butter, at room temperature
1 cup sugar, plus extra for sprinkling
1 teaspoon pure vanilla extract
3 1/2 cups all-purpose flour
1/4 teaspoon salt
6 to 7 ounces very good semisweet chocolate, finely chopped

Directions

Preheat the oven to 350 degrees F.

In the bowl of an electric mixer fitted with a paddle attachment, mix together the butter and 1 cup of sugar until they are just combined. Add the vanilla. In a medium bowl, sift together the flour and salt, then add them to the butter-and-sugar mixture. Mix on low speed until the dough starts to come together. Dump onto a surface dusted with flour and shape into a flat disk. Wrap in plastic and chill for 30 minutes.

Roll the dough 1/2-inch thick and cut with a 3 by 1-inch finger-shaped cutter. Place the cookies on a UN greased baking sheet and sprinkle with sugar. Bake for 20 to 25 minutes, until the edges begin to brown. Allow to cool to room temperature.

When the cookies are cool, place them on a baking sheet lined with parchment paper. Put 3 ounces of the chocolate in a glass bowl and microwave on high power for 30 seconds. (Don't trust your microwave timer; time it with your watch.) Stir with a wooden spoon. Continue to heat and stir in 30-second increments until the chocolate is just melted. Add the remaining chocolate and allow it to sit at room temperature, stirring often, until it's completely smooth. Stir vigorously until the chocolate is smooth and slightly cooled; stirring makes it glossier.

Brownie Cookies

Ingredients

4 ounces baking chocolate (unsweetened or bittersweet)
2 cups granulated sugar
2 sticks salted butter, softened
3 large eggs
1 tablespoon vanilla extract
2 1/4 cups all-purpose flour
1/4 cup plus 1 tablespoon cocoa powder
1 teaspoon baking powder
1/2 teaspoon kosher salt
Powdered sugar, for dusting

Directions

Preheat the oven to 350 degrees F. Line a baking sheet with a silicone baking mat or parchment paper.

Put the chocolate in a microwave-safe bowl and melt it in the microwave. Stir and let cool.

Using an electric mixer, mix together the sugar and butter in a large bowl until totally combined. With the mixer on low, slowly drizzle in the cooled chocolate. Scrape the bowl and mix again. Mix in the eggs one at a time, then the vanilla. Scrape the bowl once more and mix.

Combine the flour, cocoa powder, baking powder and salt in a bowl and stir it together. Add it in scoops to the mixing bowl with the mixer on low. Scrape the bowl once and mix one final time until all combined.

Scoop generous tablespoons of the dough onto the prepared baking sheet, then bake until the cookies are pouf y and set, 11 to 12 minutes. Let them sit on the baking sheet for 1 to 2 minutes, then remove them to a wire rack to cool completely. Repeat with the remaining dough.

Monster Cookies

Ingredients

3 eggs
1 1/4 cups packed light brown sugar
1 cup granulated sugar
1/2 teaspoon salt
1/2 teaspoon vanilla extract
1 12 -ounce jar creamy peanut butter
1 stick butter, softened
1/2 cup multi-colored chocolate candies
1/2 cup chocolate chips
1/4 cup raisins, optional
2 teaspoons baking soda
4 1/2 cups quick-cooking oatmeal (not instant)

Directions

Preheat the oven to 350 degrees F. Line cookie sheets with parchment paper or nonstick baking mats.

In a very large mixing bowl, combine the eggs and sugars. Mix well. Add the salt, vanilla, peanut butter, and butter. Mix well. Stir in the chocolate candies, chocolate chips, raisins, if using, baking soda, and oatmeal. Drop by tablespoons 2 inches apart onto the prepared cookie sheets.

Bake for 8 to 10 minutes. Do not overbake. Let stand for about 3 minutes before transferring to wire racks to cool. When cool, store in large resalable plastic bags.

Chocolate Chip Cookies

Ingredients

1/2 cup (1 stick) unsalted butter
3/4 cup packed dark brown sugar
3/4 cup sugar
2 large eggs
1 teaspoon pure vanilla extract
1 (12-ounce) bag semisweet chocolate chips, or chunks
2 1/4 cups all-purpose flour
3/4 teaspoon baking soda

1 teaspoon fine salt

Directions

Evenly position 2 racks in the middle of the oven and preheat to 375 degrees F. (on convection setting if you have it.) Line 2 baking sheets with parchment paper or silicone sheets. (If you only have 1 baking sheet, let it cool completely between batches.)
Put the butter in a microwave safe bowl, cover and microwave on medium power until melted. (Alternatively melt in a small saucepan.) Cool slightly. Whisk the sugars, eggs, butter and vanilla in a large bowl until smooth.
Whisk the flour, baking soda and salt in another bowl. Stir the dry ingredients into the wet ingredients with a wooden spoon; take care not to over mix. Stir in the chocolate chips or chunks.
Scoop heaping tablespoons of the dough onto the prepared pans. Wet hands slightly and roll the dough into balls. Space the cookies about 2-inches apart on the pans. Bake, until golden, but still soft in the center, 12 to 16 minutes, depending on how chewy or crunchy you like your cookies. Transfer hot cookies with a spatula to a rack to cool. Serve.

Rainbow Cookies

Ingredients

2 1/2 sticks unsalted butter, cut into pieces and softened, plus more for the pans
2 cups all-purpose flour, plus more for the pans
8 ounces almond paste
1 cup sugar
4 large eggs, separated
1/2 teaspoon kosher salt
Red and green food coloring (gel preferred)
1 15 -ounce jar smooth apricot jam
Cooking spray
1 pound bittersweet chocolate, chopped

Directions

You'll need three 9-by-12-inch jelly roll pans or rimmed baking sheets to make these layered cookies.
Prep the pans: Position racks in the upper and lower thirds of the oven; preheat to 350 degrees F. Butter and flour three 9-by-12-inch jelly roll pans or rimmed baking sheets and line with parchment paper.
Make the batter: Combine the almond paste and 3/4 cup plus 2 tablespoons sugar in a stand mixer fitted with the paddle attachment. Mix on medium speed until the mixture is in fine crumbles. Beat in 2 1/2 sticks butter, a few pieces at a time, until well combined. Beat in the egg yolks, one at a time, until smooth.
Sift 2 cups flour onto a sheet of parchment and sprinkle the salt on top; add to the

mixer bowl and beat until just combined.

In a clean bowl, whisk the egg whites until foamy; while whisking, slowly add the remaining 2 tablespoons sugar and whisk until firm peaks form (or use a hand mixer). Fold about one-third of the egg white mixture into the batter with a rubber spatula, then gently fold in the rest. The batter should be fluffy.

Color the batter: Divide the batter evenly among 3 bowls. Stir enough red food coloring into 1 bowl to make a deep salmon color. Stir enough green food coloring into another bowl to make a medium green color. Leave the third bowl uncolored.

Bake the layers: Transfer the batter to the prepared pans (one pan for each color). Dip an offset spatula in water and spread the batter to the edge of each pan, smoothing the tops. Bake, switching the position of the pans halfway through, until the cakes are cooked through and just beginning to brown around the edges, 8 to 10 minutes. Let cool completely in the pans on wire racks.

Assemble the layers: Spread half of the jam evenly over the green cake layer almost all the way to the edges. Unmold the plain cake layer by inverting it onto another pan or cutting board; peel off the parchment.

Carefully slide the plain layer onto the green layer (use a wide offset spatula to help you, if necessary). Spread the remaining jam on top of the plain layer. Unmold the red cake layer and slide it onto the plain layer.

Cover the cake with plastic wrap and top with one of the empty pans; place several heavy cans on top to weigh down the layers. Refrigerate at least 4 hours or overnight.

Unmold the cake: Remove the cans and plastic wrap. Place a cutting board on top of the cake and flip to unmold it onto the cutting board. Remove the parchment from the top of the green layer.

Trim the cake: Trim the sides with a knife to make straight edges. Spray a wire rack with cooking spray; set the rack over a baking sheet. Carefully slide the cake onto the rack, using a wide offset spatula to help you, if necessary.

Cover in chocolate: Melt the chocolate in a heatproof bowl set over a pan of simmering water; pour over the cake. Dip an offset spatula in the hot water and smooth the top and sides. Let set slightly. Scrape wavy lines into the chocolate with a fork; let cool a few more minutes until the chocolate is mostly set but still slightly tacky.

Cut into pieces: Slide the cake back onto the cutting board. Slice crosswise into 6 strips, then cut each strip into 8 rectangular pieces. For clean edges, dip the knife in warm water and wipe it with a cloth between cuts. Store in an airtight container at room temperature for up to 1 week.

If the lines in the chocolate don't hold their shape, let the chocolate set a little longer and try again.

Brown Sugar Oatmeal Cookies

Ingredients

2 cups packed dark brown sugar
1 cup (2 sticks) salted butter, softened
2 teaspoons vanilla extract

2 eggs
1 1/2 cups all-purpose flour
1 teaspoon salt
1/2 teaspoon baking soda
3 cups old-fashioned oats

Directions

Preheat the oven to 350 degrees F.
In the bowl of an electric mixer (or using a hand mixer), beat together the brown sugar and butter until fluffy. Beat in the vanilla. Add the eggs one at a time, scraping the bowl after each one.
Mix together the flour, salt and baking soda in a medium bowl. Add it into the creamed mixture in 2 to 3 batches, mixing until just combined. Mix in the oats until just combined.
Use your preferred size cookie scoop (or a regular spoon) to drop portions of dough onto baking sheets, spacing them a couple inches apart. Bake until dark and chewy, 12 to 13 minutes. If you'd like a crispier cookie, just cook a little longer! Let the cookies cool slightly on the baking sheets, then transfer onto a plate for serving.

'Oreo' Cookies

Ingredients

For the Dough:
1 1/3 cups Dutch-process cocoa powder
1 1/2 cups all-purpose flour, plus more for dusting
1/4 teaspoon salt
2 sticks unsalted butter, softened
2 cups granulated sugar
2 large eggs
1 teaspoon vanilla extract
For the Filling:
1 stick unsalted butter, softened
1/2 cup vegetable shortening
3 cups confectioners' sugar, sifted
1 teaspoon vanilla extract

Directions

Prepare the dough: Sift together the cocoa powder, flour and salt in a large bowl. Using a mixer, cream the butter and sugar. Add the eggs one at a time, then the vanilla, incorporating each ingredient before adding the next. Add the dry ingredients and mix just until incorporated, scraping the bottom of the bowl with a rubber spatula.
Divide the dough into 2 pieces; place one piece between 2 lightly floured sheets of

parchment paper and roll into a 1/4-inch-thick rectangle. Repeat with the other piece of dough. Refrigerate both rectangles, covered with the parchment sheets, until firm, at least 1 hour or up to several days.

Using a 2-inch round cutter, cut the dough into 64 circles. (You can reroll the scraps once.) Place the cookies about 2 inches apart on ungreased baking sheets and chill for 20 minutes. Preheat the oven to 325 degrees.

Bake the cookies until they are set and slightly darker around the edges, about 20 minutes. Cool completely on wire racks.

Meanwhile, prepare the filling: Using a mixer, cream the butter and shortening until fluffy. Beat in the confectioners' sugar and vanilla.

Flip half of the cookies upside down and top each with 1 level tablespoon of filling. Press the remaining cookies on top to make sandwiches.

Flourless Peanut Butter Cookies

Ingredients

1 cup natural peanut butter
1 cup sugar
1 teaspoon pure vanilla extract
1 large egg, lightly beaten
coarse sea salt, for sprinkling

Directions

Preheat the oven to 350 degrees F and place the racks in the upper and lower third of the oven.

In a medium bowl, mix the peanut butter, sugar, vanilla and egg until well combined. Spoon 1 tablespoon of the mixture about 1 inch apart onto UN greased baking sheets. Flatten the mounds with the tines of a fork, making a crosshatch pattern on the cookies. Sprinkle coarse salt on top of the cookies.

Bake until golden around the edges, about 10 minutes, switching the position of the sheets halfway through baking. Transfer to racks to cool. Repeat with the remaining dough.

From Food Network Kitchens; after further testing and to ensure the best results this recipe has been altered from what was in the actual episode.

Glazed Limon cello Cookies

Ingredients

Cookies:

3/4 cup (1 1/2 sticks) salted butter, softened
3/4 cup granulated sugar
2 large egg yolks, at room temperature
1/2 teaspoon vanilla extract

2 teaspoons freshly grated lemon zest (about 1 medium lemon)
2 cups all-purpose flour

Glaze:

1 cup confectioners' sugar
2 tablespoons Limon cello
1 teaspoon freshly grated lemon zest
1 tablespoon freshly squeezed lemon juice

Directions

For the cookies:
  Preheat the oven to 350 degrees F. Line 2 baking sheets with parchment paper and set aside.
Using an electric mixer, beat the butter and granulated sugar until the mixture is light and fluffy. Add the egg yolks, vanilla and zest, and beat until combined. Add the flour to the mixture, a little at a time, until a soft dough forms.
Divide the dough in half and, using your hands, shape it into 2 logs, each 2 inches in diameter. Wrap the logs in waxed paper and refrigerate until firm, about 30 minutes, or place in the freezer for 15 minutes. Cut the logs into 1/4-inch-thick slices and place them on the prepared baking sheets about 2 inches apart.
Bake the cookies for 15 to 18 minutes, or until the edges are slightly browned. Remove from the oven and allow to cool on the baking sheets for 10 minutes.
For the glaze: Meanwhile, in a small bowl, whisk together the confectioners' sugar, Limon cello, lemon zest and lemon juice. Dip the top of each cookie into the glaze, and place the cookies on a cooling rack set over the baking sheets. Allow to set for about 15 minutes before serving. Store in an airtight container for up to 2 weeks.

Compost Cookies

Ingredients

1/2 cup old-fashioned rolled oats
1/2 cup Rice Chex cereal
2 tablespoons unsalted butter, melted, plus 10 tablespoons (1 1/4 sticks) unsalted butter, at room temperature
3/4 teaspoon plus 1/8 teaspoon kosher salt
1 cup all-purpose flour
2 teaspoons ground coffee
3/4 teaspoon baking soda
3/4 cup granulated sugar
1/2 cup packed dark brown sugar
1 large egg
2 teaspoons pure vanilla extract
1/2 cup chopped bittersweet chocolate (around 60 percent cacao)
1/2 cup honey-roasted peanuts, coarsely chopped

1/2 cup dried sour cherries, chopped
1/2 cup lightly crushed salted potato chips
Flaky sea salt, for sprinkling

Directions

Preheat the oven to 350 degrees F.
In a medium bowl, toss together the oats, Chex cereal, the 2 tablespoons melted butter and 1/8 teaspoon of the salt. Spread the mixture onto a baking sheet and bake until deep golden brown and fragrant, about 10 minutes, stirring halfway through the baking time.
In a medium bowl, whisk together the flour, coffee, baking soda and remaining 3/4 teaspoon salt. In a large bowl, using a wooden spoon, mix together the 10 tablespoons room-temperature butter, granulated sugar and brown sugar until creamy. Stir in the egg and vanilla. Then carefully fold in the chocolate, peanuts, sour cherries, potato chips and the oat and Chex mixture. Scoop the dough into 2-tablespoon scoops and roll each one into a neat ball. Freeze the dough balls for at least 1 hour.
Preheat the oven to 325 degrees F.
Set the dough balls at least 3 inches apart on parchment-lined baking sheets and sprinkle with the flaky sea salt. Bake until the cookies are golden brown and the centers are just set, 18 to 22 minutes, rotating the sheets halfway through. Let the cookies cool on the baking sheets for 10 minutes, then transfer to a rack to cool completely.

Fruitcake Cookies

Ingredients

1/2 pound dried figs
1/4 pound raisins
2 ounces candied cherries, coarsely chopped
2 ounces dried apricots, coarsely chopped
1 tablespoon honey
2 tablespoons dry sherry
1 tablespoon freshly squeezed lemon juice
6 ounces chopped pecans
Kosher salt
1/2 pound (2 sticks) unsalted butter, at room temperature
1/2 teaspoon ground cloves
1/2 cup superfine sugar
1/3 cup light brown sugar, firmly packed
1 extra-large egg
2 2/3 cups all-purpose flour

Directions

Snip off the hard stems of the figs with scissors or a small knife and coarsely chop the figs. In a medium bowl, combine the figs, raisins, cherries, apricots, honey, sherry, lemon juice, pecans, and a pinch of salt. Cover with plastic wrap and allow to sit overnight at room temperature.

In the bowl of an electric mixer fitted with the paddle attachment, cream the butter, cloves, superfine sugar, and brown sugar on medium speed until smooth, about 3 minutes. With the mixer on low speed, add the egg and mix until incorporated. With the mixer still on low, slowly add the flour and 1/4 teaspoon salt just until combined. Don't over mix! Add the fruits and nuts, including any liquid in the bowl.

Divide the dough in half and place each half on the long edge of a 12 by 18-inch piece of parchment or waxed paper. Roll each half into a log, 1 1/2 to 1 3/4-inch thick, making an 18-inch-long roll. Refrigerate the dough for several hours, or until firm.

Ginger Cookies

Ingredients

3/4 cup vegetable shortening
1 cup sugar, plus more for rolling
1 large egg
1/4 cup molasses
2 cups sifted all-purpose flour
2 teaspoons baking soda
1 teaspoon ground cinnamon
1 teaspoon ground ginger
1/2 teaspoon ground cloves
1/2 teaspoon salt

Directions

Preheat the oven to 350 degrees F.

Line cookie sheets with parchment paper or nonstick baking mats. Using an electric mixer at low speed, cream the shortening and sugar until thoroughly combined. Add the egg and molasses and beat until completely incorporated. Sift together the flour, baking soda, cinnamon, ginger, cloves and salt and add to the mixture. Stir until combined. Roll the dough into balls about 1-inch in diameter. Roll the balls in sugar. Place 1/2-inch apart on the prepared cookie sheets. Flatten the balls slightly with your fingertips. Bake for 12 minutes. Cool on wire racks.

Cowboy Cookie

Ingredients

1 cup shortening (recommended: Crisco)

1 cup granulated sugar
1 cup brown sugar
2 eggs
1 teaspoon vanilla extract
2 cups all-purpose flour
1 teaspoon baking soda
1/2 teaspoon salt
1/2 teaspoon baking powder
2 cups rolled oats
1/2 cup chopped pecans
1 (6-ounce) package chocolate chips
1/2 cup shredded coconut

Directions

Preheat oven to 350 degrees F.
In a large bowl, with an electric mixer, cream the shortening, granulated sugar, and brown sugar. Add eggs and the vanilla and beat until well blended. Stir in the flour, baking soda, salt, and baking powder. Add oats, nuts, chocolate chips and coconut, mix until combined. Spoon cookie mixture onto greased foil lined cookie sheet. Bake for 8 to 10 minutes. Transfer the cookies to a wire rack to cool.

Gluten free cookie

Ingredients

One 15-ounce can gluten-free almond paste, finely crumbled
1 cup confectioners' sugar
2 tablespoons honey
Pinch ground cinnamon
Pinch fine salt
2 large egg whites
1 lemon, zested
1/2 to 3/4 cups pine nuts
Special Equipment: disposable pastry bag
Directions

Preheat the oven to 350 degrees F. Line sheet trays with parchment paper or silicone baking mats.
In the bowl of a stand mixer equipped with the paddle attachment, beat the almond paste on high speed until it is really broken up. Add the confectioners' sugar and mix on slow speed until well combined.
Add the honey, cinnamon, salt, egg whites and lemon zest and beat on medium speed until the mixture is well combined and very thick, about 5 minutes.
Fill a disposable pastry bag with the dough. Push the dough towards the tip and cut the tip off the bag. Pipe 1-inch balls onto the prepared sheet trays. Top with the pine nuts, pressing them into the dough to secure. Bake until the cookies are

golden, 12 to 14 minutes.

Chocolate Chip Oatmeal Cookies

Ingredients

1 cup all-purpose flour
1/2 teaspoon baking powder
1/2 teaspoon baking soda
1/4 teaspoon salt
2 cups rolled (old-fashioned) oats
1/2 cup coarsely chopped pecans
8 tablespoons (1 stick) unsalted butter, at room temperature
1/2 cup lightly packed light brown sugar
1/2 cup granulated sugar
1 large egg
1/4 cup maple syrup
1/2 teaspoon vanilla extract
3/4 cup semisweet chocolate chips

Directions

Set 2 racks in the middle and upper thirds of the oven and preheat to 350 degrees
F.
In a medium bowl, stir the flour, baking powder, baking soda, salt, oats, and
pecans together with a whisk or fork.
In a large bowl, beat the butter, brown sugar, and granulated sugar together for
30 seconds until blended. Beat in the egg until smooth and barely fluffy. With
mixer running on medium high, drizzle in the maple syrup, and vanilla until
incorporated. Turn the mixer down to its lowest setting and gradually add the
flour-oatmeal mixture. Blend just to combine, then mix in the chocolate chips.
Drop walnut-sized balls of dough onto a nonstick or parchment-lined cookie
sheet at 3-inch intervals. With moistened fingers, flatten and round out the
cookies a little. Bake for 9 minutes, turning the pan once for even baking. The
cookies are done when they are lightly browned on top. Set the cookie sheets on a
rack to cool.

Lemon Ricotta

Ingredients

Cookies:

2 1/2 cups all-purpose flour
1 teaspoon baking powder
1 teaspoon salt

1 stick unsalted butter, softened
2 cups sugar
2 eggs
1 (15-ounce) container whole milk ricotta cheese
3 tablespoons lemon juice
1 lemon, zested

Glaze:

1 1/2 cups powdered sugar
3 tablespoons lemon juice
1 lemon, zested

Directions

Preheat the oven to 375 degrees F.
Cookies:

In a medium bowl combine the flour, baking powder, and salt. Set aside.
In the large bowl combine the butter and the sugar. Using an electric mixer beat the butter and sugar until light and fluffy, about 3 minutes. Add the eggs, 1 at a time, beating until incorporated. Add the ricotta cheese, lemon juice, and lemon zest. Beat to combine. Stir in the dry ingredients.
Line 2 baking sheets with parchment paper. Spoon the dough (about 2 tablespoons for each cookie) onto the baking sheets. Bake for 15 minutes, until slightly golden at the edges. Remove from the oven and let the cookies rest on the baking sheet for 20 minutes.

Glaze:

Combine the powdered sugar, lemon juice, and lemon zest in a small bowl and stir until smooth. Spoon about 1/2-teaspoon onto each cookie and use the back of the spoon to gently spread. Let the glaze harden for about 2 hours. Pack the cookies into a decorative container.

Fortune Cookies

Ingredients

2 egg whites, room temperature
6 tablespoons butter
1/4 cup sugar
1/2 cup flour, sifted
1/4 teaspoons vanilla extract

Directions

Cut a stencil out of a plastic coffee can lid in the shape of a 3-inch disk. Whip the egg whites until stiff and chill. In a mixer, cream the butter, then add the sugar and continue mixing. Add the flour and blend in, then add the vanilla and blend again. Add the chilled egg whites and mix on low until well incorporated and the batter is smooth. With a small offset spatula, spread batter through the stencil so it is a circle onto a slat or parchment paper, about 6 per cookie sheet. Bake in a preheated 350-degree oven until light golden brown, 7 to 8 minutes. Quickly remove the pan from the oven and one at time place a fortune across the center with a bit hanging out. Fold cookie circle in thirds over fortune with flaps only slightly overlapping each other. Turn over and bring opposing sides together and pinch. Let cool.

Chocolate No-Bake Cookies

Ingredients

2 cups sugar
1/2 cup milk
1 stick (8 tablespoons) unsalted butter
1/4 cup unsweetened cocoa powder
3 cups old-fashioned rolled oats
1 cup smooth peanut butter
1 tablespoon pure vanilla extract
Large pinch kosher salt

Directions

Line a baking sheet with wax paper or parchment.
Bring the sugar, milk, butter and cocoa to a boil in a medium saucepan over medium heat, stirring occasionally, then let boil for 1 minute. Remove from the heat. Add the oats, peanut butter, vanilla and salt, and stir to combine.
Drop teaspoonful of the mixture onto the prepared baking sheet, and let sit at room temperature until cooled and hardened, about 30 minutes. Refrigerate in an airtight container for up to 3 days.

Raisin Pecan Oatmeal Cookies

Ingredients

1 1/2 cups pecans
1/2 pound (2 sticks) unsalted butter, at room temperature
1 cup dark brown sugar, lightly packed
1 cup granulated sugar
2 extra-large eggs, at room temperature
2 teaspoons pure vanilla extract

1 1/2 cups all-purpose flour
1 teaspoon baking powder
1 teaspoon ground cinnamon
1 teaspoon kosher salt
3 cups old-fashioned oatmeal
1 1/2 cups raisins

Directions

Preheat the oven to 350 degrees F.
Place the pecans on a sheet pan and bake for 5 minutes, until crisp. Set aside to cool. Chop very coarsely.
In the bowl of an electric mixer fitted with the paddle attachment, beat the butter, brown sugar, and granulated sugar together on medium-high speed until light and fluffy. With the mixer on low, add the eggs, one at a time, and the vanilla. Sift the flour, baking powder, cinnamon, and salt together into a medium bowl. With the mixer on low, slowly add the dry ingredients to the butter mixture. Add the oats, raisins, and pecans and mix just until combined.
Using a small ice-cream scoop or a tablespoon, drop 2-inch mounds of dough onto sheet pans lined with parchment paper. Flatten slightly with a damp hand. Bake for 12 to 15 minutes, until lightly browned. Transfer the cookies to a baking rack and cool completely.

Oatmeal Cookies

Ingredients

1 cup all-purpose flour
3/4 teaspoon baking soda
1/2 teaspoon fine salt
1/2 teaspoon ground allspice
1/2 teaspoon ground cinnamon
1/8 teaspoon ground mace
3/4 cup unsalted butter, at room temperature
1/2 cup sugar
3/4 cup packed light brown sugar
2 large eggs, at room temperature
1 teaspoon vanilla extract, at room temperature
2 3/4 cups rolled oats
3/4 cup raisins
3/4 cup chopped pecans

Directions

Position the racks in the top and lower third of the oven and preheat to 350 degrees F.

In a large bowl, whisk together the flour, baking soda, salt, allspice, cinnamon, and mace.

In another large bowl, combine the butter and sugar and, with a hand-held electric mixer, mix on low speed until just incorporated. Raise the speed to high and mix until light and fluffy. (Occasionally turn the mixer off, and scrape the sides of the bowl down with a rubber spatula.)

Add the brown sugar and mix until incorporated. Add the eggs to the butter mixture, one at time, and waiting for the first one to be fully incorporated before adding the last. Mix in the vanilla.

Reduce the mixer's speed to low. Add the flour mixture, little by little, until a smooth dough is formed (scrape the bowl down occasionally). Turn off the machine, stir in the oats, raisins, and pecans with a rubber spatula.

Line 2 baking sheets with parchment paper. Using a spoon, drop heaping tablespoons of the dough onto the sheets, spaced about 2 inches apart.

Bake the cookies in batches, turning the pans once, until golden brown, but still soft and spongy, about 15 minutes per batch. Let the cookies cool slightly on the baking sheets, and then transfer to racks to cool completely. Store in a sealed container.

Meringue Cookies

Ingredients

2 large egg whites, at room temperature
1/2 teaspoon cream of tartar
2/3 cup superfine granulated sugar
1 teaspoon vanilla extract
1 cup semisweet chocolate chips or finely chopped semisweet chocolate
1 cup finely chopped walnuts

Directions

Preheat the oven to 350 degrees F and line 2 baking sheets with parchment paper. Set aside.

In the bowl of an electric mixer, beat egg whites until foamy. Add the cream of tartar and beat until fluffy but not at all dry. (Be careful not to over beat.) Add the sugar gradually, about 3 tablespoons at a time. When 1/2 of the sugar has been added, add the vanilla extract. Continue beating and adding remaining sugar in batches, until all of the sugar is dissolved and the meringue is very shiny and tight. Gently fold in the chocolate chips and chopped nuts. Working one teaspoon at a time, push a teaspoonful of meringue from the tip of 1 teaspoon with the back of another teaspoon onto the lined baking sheets, leaving 1-inch of space between cookies. Place baking sheets in the preheated oven and turn the oven off. Leave the cookies (undisturbed) in the oven for at least 2 hours and up to overnight, or until cookies are crisp and dry.

Chewy Chocolate Chip Cookies

Ingredients

2 3/4 cups all-purpose flour
1 teaspoon salt
1 teaspoon baking powder
1 teaspoon baking soda
2 1/2 sticks unsalted butter, softened
1 3/4 cups packed dark brown sugar
1/4 cup granulated sugar
2 large eggs, at room temperature
2 teaspoons vanilla extract
2 cups semisweet chocolate chips

Directions

Sift the flour, salt, baking powder and baking soda together into a large bowl. Beat the butter, brown sugar and granulated sugar in a bowl with a mixer on medium-high speed until pale and fluffy, about 4 minutes (use the paddle attachment for a stand mixer). Beat in the eggs one at a time, then beat in the vanilla. Reduce the mixer speed to low. Add the flour mixture and beat until combined. Stir in the chocolate chips by hand. Press plastic wrap directly onto the surface of the dough and refrigerate at least 1 hour or preferably overnight. Preheat the oven to 375 degrees F. Line 2 baking sheets with parchment paper. Drop heaping tablespoonful's of dough onto the prepared baking sheets, about 2 inches apart. Bake until the cookies are golden around the edges but still soft in the middle, about 12 minutes. Remove the cookies from the oven and let cool 10 minutes on the baking sheets, then transfer to racks to cool completely.

Cheesecake Cookies

Ingredients

1 1/4 cups finely crushed graham crackers (1 sleeve)
1 cup flour
1 1/2 teaspoons baking powder
1 stick (8 tablespoons) unsalted butter, softened
1/2 cup packed brown sugar
1 egg, separated
3 ounces cream cheese, softened
1/4 cup granulated sugar
2 teaspoons lemon zest
1/2 teaspoon vanilla extract

Directions

Preheat the oven to 350 degrees F.

In a large bowl, stir together the graham cracker crumbs, flour and baking powder. In a medium bowl, beat together the butter with the brown sugar using an electric hand mixer. Add the egg white and beat until well combined. Add to the graham cracker crumbs and blend until just combined.

In a separate medium bowl, beat together the softened cream cheese with the granulated sugar, egg yolk, lemon zest and vanilla until well combined. Set aside. Using a small ice cream scoop, scoop out the cookie dough and place on a nonstick or parchment lined baking sheet. (If you do not have an ice scoop, then measure out the dough into scoops of about 2 tablespoons.) Flatten slightly, pressing your thumb in the center of the ball to create a small bowl shape. Repeat with the remaining dough. Spoon the cream cheese into the indents in the cookies. Bake until the filling is barely set and the cookies are lightly golden, 12 minutes. Allow to cool 5 minutes on the baking sheets before removing them and cooling completely on a wire rack.

Chewy Sugar Cookies

Ingredients

2 3/4 cups all-purpose flour
1 teaspoon baking soda
1/2 teaspoon baking powder
1 cup softened butter
1 1/2 cups white sugar
1 egg
1 teaspoon vanilla extract
3 to 4 tablespoons buttermilk
Sprinkles or colored sugar, for decorating

Directions

Preheat oven to 375 degrees F.

In a small bowl, stir together flour, baking soda, and baking powder. Set aside. In a large bowl, cream together butter and sugar until smooth. Beat in the egg and vanilla. Gradually blend in dry ingredients. Add enough of the buttermilk to moisten the dough and make it soft, not wet.

Roll rounded teaspoons of dough into balls and place on an ungreased cookie sheet. With a brush or fingers, moisten the top of each cookie with the remaining buttermilk and slightly flatten the top of each cookie. Sprinkle with raw sugar or colored sprinkles.

Chocolate Pecan Skillet Cookie

Ingredients

1 1/2 sticks (12 tablespoons) unsalted butter
1 cup packed light brown sugar
1 cup granulated sugar
1 tablespoon pure vanilla extract
2 large eggs, beaten
2 cups all-purpose flour (see Cook's Note)
1/2 cup unsweetened cocoa powder
1 teaspoon fine salt
3/4 teaspoon baking soda
2 cups pecan halves (8 ounces), roughly chopped
Vanilla ice cream, for serving, optional

Directions

Position an oven rack in the center of the oven and preheat to 350 degrees F.
Melt the butter in a 10-inch cast-iron skillet over medium heat, 2 to 3 minutes,
then set aside to cool 5 minutes. Whisk the brown sugar, granulated sugar, vanilla
and eggs in a large bowl until smooth. Pour in the butter from the skillet and
whisk until combined. Do not wipe out the skillet.
Whisk the flour, cocoa powder, salt and baking soda in a medium bowl. Stir the
flour mixture into the egg mixture with a rubber spatula until just incorporated,
being careful not to over mix. Stir in all but 1/4 cup of the pecans.
Scrape the dough into the buttered skillet, gently spreading it to the edges and
making the top even. Sprinkle the remaining 1/4 cup pecans on top and press
lightly with the rubber spatula to make them stick to the dough. Bake until the
top is cracked, the edges are slightly browned and crisp and the center is still soft
when gently pressed, 40 to 45 minutes. Cool in the skillet on a wire rack for 15
minutes. Cut into wedges and serve warm with ice cream if desired.

Molasses Cookies

Ingredients

2 1/2 cups all-purpose flour
2 teaspoons baking soda
1 teaspoon ground cinnamon
1 teaspoon ground ginger
1/2 teaspoon ground cloves
Pinch kosher salt
1 1/2 sticks (12 tablespoons) unsalted butter, at room temperature
1 cup brown sugar
1 large egg
3/4 cup molasses
Turbinate sugar, for coating

Directions

preheat the oven to 350 degrees F.

In a medium bowl, combine the flour, baking soda, cinnamon, ginger, cloves and salt and set aside.

In the bowl of a standing mixer fitted with the paddle attachment, cream together the butter and brown sugar until light and fluffy. Beat in the egg and then the molasses. In thirds, gently mix in the flour mixture until just combined.

Using an ice cream scoop, scoop out the cookie dough into 1-inch balls onto a sheet tray covered with turbinate sugar. Gently toss the dough balls in the sugar, covering them completely. Place the sugar-coated dough balls on another sheet tray and gently squish a little.

Chocolate Chunk Cookies

Ingredients

1/2 pound unsalted butter, at room temperature
1 cup light brown sugar, packed
1/2 cup granulated sugar
2 teaspoons pure vanilla extract
2 extra-large eggs, at room temperature
2 cups all-purpose flour
1 teaspoon baking soda
1 teaspoon kosher salt
1 1/2 cups chopped walnuts
1 1/4 pounds semisweet chocolate chunks

Directions

Preheat the oven to 350 degrees.

Cream the butter and two sugars until light and fluffy in the bowl of an electric mixer fitted with the paddle attachment. Add the vanilla, then the eggs, one at a time, and mix well. Sift together the flour, baking soda, and salt and add to the butter with the mixer on low speed, mixing only until combined. Fold in the walnuts and chocolate chunks.

Drop the dough on a baking sheet lined with parchment paper, using a 1 3/4-inch-diameter ice cream scoop or a rounded tablespoon. Dampen your hands and flatten the dough slightly. Bake for exactly 15 minutes (the cookies will seem underdone). Remove from the oven and let cool slightly on the pan, then transfer to a wire rack to cool completely.

Pumpkin Chocolate Chip Cookies

Ingredients

1 cup (2 sticks) unsalted butter, softened

1 cup white sugar
1 cup light brown sugar
2 large eggs
1 teaspoon vanilla extract
1 cup canned pumpkin puree
3 cups all-purpose flour
2 teaspoons baking soda
1/2 teaspoon salt
1 teaspoon ground cinnamon
1/2 teaspoon ground ginger
1/4 teaspoon ground nutmeg
1/4 teaspoon ground cloves
2 cups (12-ounce bag) milk chocolate chips, not semisweet
Nonstick cooking spray or parchment paper

Directions

Heat the oven to 350 degrees F. Spray cookie sheets with nonstick spray or line them with parchment paper.
Using a mixer, beat the butter until smooth. Beat in the white and brown sugars, a little at a time, until the mixture is light and fluffy. Beat in the eggs 1 at a time, then mix in the vanilla and pumpkin puree. In a large bowl, whisk together the flour, baking soda, salt, cinnamon, ginger, nutmeg, and cloves. Slowly beat the flour mixture into the batter in thirds. Stir in the chips. Scoop the cookie dough by heaping tablespoons onto the prepared cookie sheets and bake for 15 to 20 minutes, or until the cookies are browned around the edges. Remove the cookie sheets from the oven and let them rest for 2 minutes. Take the cookies off with a spatula and cool them on wire racks.

Gingerbread Cookies 101

Ingredients

3 cups all-purpose flour
1 teaspoon baking soda
3/4 teaspoon ground cinnamon
3/4 teaspoon ground ginger
1/2 teaspoon ground allspice
1/2 teaspoon ground cloves
1/2 teaspoon salt
1/4 teaspoon freshly milled black pepper
8 tablespoons (1 stick) unsalted butter, at room temperature
1/4 cup vegetable shortening, at room temperature
1/2 cup packed light brown sugar
2/3 cup un sulfured molasses
1 large egg

ROYAL ICING

1 pound (4 1/2 cups) confectioners' sugar
2 tablespoons dried egg-white powder
6 tablespoons water

Directions

Position the racks in the top and bottom thirds of the oven and preheat to 350 degrees F.

Sift the flour, baking soda, cinnamon, ginger, allspice, cloves, salt and pepper through a wire sieve into a medium bowl. Set aside.

In a large bowl, using a hand-held electric mixer at high speed, beat the butter and vegetable shortening until well-combined, about 1 minute. Add the brown sugar and beat until the mixture is light in texture and color, about 2 minutes. Beat in the molasses and egg. Using a wooden spoon, gradually mix in the flour mixture to make a stiff dough. Divide the dough into two thick disks and wrap each disk in plastic wrap. Refrigerate until chilled, about 3 hours. (The dough can be prepared up to 2 days ahead.)

To roll out the cookies, work with one disk at a time, keeping the other disk refrigerated. Remove the dough from the refrigerator and let stand at room temperature until just warm enough to roll out without cracking, about 10 minutes. (If the dough has been chilled for longer than 3 hours, it may need a few more minutes.) Place the dough on a lightly floured work surface and sprinkle the top of the dough with flour. Roll out the dough 1/8 inch thick, being sure that the dough isn't sticking to the work surface (run a long metal spatula or knife under the dough occasionally just to be sure, and dust the surface with more flour, if needed). For softer cookies, roll out slightly thicker. Using cookie cutters, cut out the cookies and transfer to nonstick cookie sheets, placing the cookies 1 inch apart. Gently knead the scraps together and form into another disk. Wrap and chill for 5 minutes before rolling out again to cut out more cookies.

Bake, switching the positions of the cookies from top to bottom and back to front halfway through baking, until the edges of the cookies are set and crisp, 10 to 12 minutes. Cool on the sheets for 2 minutes, then transfer to wire cake racks to cool completely. Decorate with Royal Icing. (The cookies can be prepared up to 1 week ahead, stored in airtight containers at room temperature.)

ROYAL ICING

Make ahead: The icing can prepared up to 2 days ahead, stored in an airtight container with a moist paper towel pressed directly on the icing surface, and refrigerated.

This icing hardens into shiny white lines, and is used for piping decorations on gingerbread people or other cookies. Traditional royal icing uses raw egg whites, but I prefer dried egg-white powder, available at most supermarkets, to avoid any concern about uncooked egg whites.

When using a pastry bag, practice your decorating skills before you ice the cookies. Just do a few trial runs to get the feel of the icing and the bag, piping the icing onto aluminum foil or wax paper. If you work quickly, you can use a metal spatula to scrape the test icing back into the batch.

Dried egg-white powder is also available by mail order from The Baker's Catalogue, 1-800-827-6836. Meringue powder, which is dehydrated egg whites with sugar already added, also makes excellent royal icing; just follow the directions on the package. However, the plain unsweetened dried egg whites are more versatile, as they can be used in savory dishes, too. Meringue powder is available from Adventures in Cooking (1-800-305-1114) and The Baker's Catalogue.

In a medium bowl, using a hand-held electric mixer at low speed, beat the confectioners' sugar, egg-white powder and water until combined. Increase the speed to high and beat, scraping down the sides of the bowl often, until very stiff, shiny and thick enough to pipe; 3 to 5 minutes. (The icing can be prepared up to 2 days ahead, stored in an airtight container with a moist paper towel pressed directly on the icing surface, and refrigerated.)

To pipe line decorations, use a pastry bag fitted with a tube with a small writing tip about 1/8-inch wide, such as ATECO No. 7; it may be too difficult to squeeze the icing out of smaller tips. If necessary, thin the icing with a little warm water. To fill the pastry bag, fit it with the tube. Fold the top of the bag back to form a cuff and hold it in one hand. (Or, place the bag in a tall glass and fold the top back to form a cuff.) Using a rubber spatula, scoop the icing into the bag. Unfold the cuff and twist the top of the bag closed. Squeeze the icing down to fill the tube. Always practice first on a sheet of wax paper or aluminum foil to check the flow and consistency of the icing.

Traditional Royal Icing: Substitute 3 large egg whites for the powder and water.

White Chocolate Cranberry Cookies

Ingredients

1/2 cup unsalted butter, softened
1/2 cup packed light brown sugar
1/2 cup granulated sugar
1 tablespoon vanilla extract
1 large egg
1 1/2 cups all-purpose flour
1 1/2 teaspoons baking soda
1 cup dried cranberries, chopped
3/4 cup white chocolate chips
3/4 cup macadamia nuts, chopped

Directions

Preheat the oven to 350 degrees F. Line 2 baking sheet with parchment paper. With an electric mixer, cream the butter and both sugars together until smooth. Add the vanilla and egg, mixing well. Sift together the flour and baking soda.

Spoon the flour mixture gradually into the creamed sugar mixture. Stir in the cranberries, white chocolate chips and macadamia nuts. Drop by heaping spoonful's, about 2 tablespoons, onto the prepared baking sheets, 2 inches apart. Bake one sheet at a time until lightly golden on top and the edges are set, 12 to 15 minutes. Cool on the sheet about 5 minutes, and then transfer to a wire rack to cool completely. Store in an airtight container for up to 2 weeks.

Cinnamon Cookies

Ingredients

2 cups all-purpose flour
1 teaspoon baking soda
1/2 teaspoon salt
1 teaspoon ground cinnamon
1 teaspoon ground cloves
1 teaspoon ground ginger
3/4 cup solid shortening, such a Crisco
1 1/2 cups sugar
1/4 cup molasses
1 large egg

Directions

Preheat the oven to 350 degrees F.
On a large piece of waxed paper, sift together the flour, baking soda, salt, cinnamon, cloves and ginger.
Cream the shortening and 1 cup of the sugar in a stand mixer fitted with the paddle attachment. Add the flour mixture and mix to combine. Mix in the molasses and the egg. Cover the dough in plastic wrap and chill until firm, 1 hour. Roll the dough into 1-inch balls. Roll the dough balls in the remaining 1/2 cup sugar and place on a UN greased cookie sheet, spaced 1- to 1 1/2-inches apart. Bake for 20 minutes. Transfer the cookies to a wire rack to cool. Store in an airtight container.

Oatmeal Cranberry Cookies

Ingredients

1 cup unsalted butter
3/4 cup granulated sugar
3/4 cup brown sugar
2 eggs
1 teaspoon pure vanilla extract
1 1/2 cups flour
1/2 teaspoon salt

1 teaspoon baking soda
1 teaspoon cinnamon
1/2 teaspoon nutmeg
1/4 teaspoon cardamom
3 cups rolled oats
1 cup dried cranberries (or other dried fruit)

Directions

Preheat oven to 350 degrees. Cream butter and sugars until fluffy. Add eggs and vanilla. Combine dry ingredients. Add to butter mixture and stir until well blended. Add dried cranberries. Drop by teaspoonful onto parchment covered baking sheet. Bake about 10 to 12 minutes, or until lightly golden. Cool.

Lentil Cookies

Ingredients

9 1/2 ounces whole-wheat pastry flour, approximately 2 cups*
1 teaspoon baking powder
1 teaspoon salt
1 1/2 teaspoons ground cinnamon
1/2 teaspoon ground allspice
8 ounces sugar, approximately 1 cup
6 ounces unsalted butter, room temperature, approximately 3/4 cup
1 egg
2 teaspoons vanilla extract
1 1/2 cups lentil puree, recipe follows
3 1/2 ounces rolled oats, approximately 1 cup
4 ounces dried fruit, approximately 1 cup
2 1/4 ounces unsweetened dried shredded coconut, approximately 1 cup

Lentil Puree:

4 ounces lentils, approximately 2/3 cup, picked over and rinsed
2 cups water

Directions

If desired, a quarter of the whole-wheat flour can be substituted with lentil flour for a denser, stronger flavored cookie
Preheat the oven to 375 degrees F.
In a medium bowl, combine the flour, baking powder, salt, cinnamon and allspice. In the bowl of a stand-mixer with a whisk attachment, cream together the sugar and butter on medium speed. Add the egg and mix until just incorporated. Add the vanilla and lentil puree and mix until combined. Add the flour mixture and blend on low speed until just combined. Remove the bowl from the mixer and stir

in the oats, dried fruit and coconut.

Form the dough into balls about 2 teaspoons in size and place on a baking sheet with parchment paper, leaving about 1-inch of room in between. Bake for 15 to 17 minutes, or until an internal temperature of 195 degrees F is reached on an instant-read thermometer.

Lentil Puree:

In a small pot over medium heat, combine the lentils and the water. Bring to a simmer, cover, and simmer for 30 to 40 minutes, or until lentils are tender. Remove from the heat and puree. If using immediately, let cool. The puree may be stored in the refrigerator for 3 to 4 days or in the freezer for 2 to 3 months.

Earl Grey Shortbread Cookies

Ingredients

2 cups all-purpose flour
2 tablespoons loose Earl Grey tea leaves
1/2 teaspoon salt
3/4 cup confectioners' sugar
1 teaspoon pure vanilla extract
1 cup (2 sticks) butter, room temperature

Directions

In a food processor, pulse together the flour, tea, and salt, until the tea is just spotted throughout the flour. Add the confectioners' sugar, vanilla, and butter. Pulse together just until a dough is formed. Place dough on a sheet of plastic wrap, and roll into a log, about 2 1/2-inches in diameter. Tightly twist each end of wrap, and chill in refrigerator for 30 minutes.

Preheat oven to 375 degrees F.

Slice the log into 1/3-inch thick disks. Place on parchment or slat lined baking sheets, 2 inches apart (2 probably needed depending on size of sheets). Bake until the edges are just brown, about 12 minutes. Let cool on sheets for 5 minutes, then transfer to wire racks and cool to room temperature.

Ground Walnut Cookies

Ingredients

1 cup (2 sticks) unsalted butter, at room temperature
1/2 cup sugar
2 cups all-purpose flour
1/2 cup ground walnuts
1 cup chopped walnuts
1/2 cup powdered sugar, plus more for serving

Directions

Using an electric mixer, beat the butter in a large bowl until light and fluffy. Add the sugar and beat until well blended. Beat in the flour, and then the ground and chopped walnuts. Divide the dough in half, forming each half into a ball. Wrap separately in plastic and chill until cold, about 30 minutes.

Preheat the oven to 325 degrees F.

Working with half of the chilled dough at a time while keeping the rest in the fridge, roll the dough by 2 teaspoonful between your palms into balls. Arrange the balls on a large baking sheet, spacing them 1/2-inch apart.

Bake the cookies until golden brown on the bottom and just pale golden on top, about 18 minutes. Cool the cookies for 5 minutes on the baking sheet. Toss the warm cookies in the powdered sugar. Transfer the sugar-coated cookies to a rack to cool completely. (The cookies can be prepared 2 days ahead. Store in an airtight container at room temperature). Sift additional powdered sugar over the cookies, if desired, before serving.

Chewy Truffle Cookies

Ingredients

1 cup dried pitted dates, 4-ounces, chopped
1 cup water
1 tablespoon fresh lemon juice
2 tablespoons honey or agave syrup
2 tablespoons reduced-fat or no-stir natural chunky peanut butter
2 tablespoons unsweetened cocoa powder
1 tablespoon unsalted butter
1/4 teaspoon kosher salt
8 full sheets whole wheat graham crackers, finely ground, about 1 1/4 cups
1/2 cup old-fashioned rolled oats, not instant
Cooking spray
For coating: unsweetened coconut flakes, crushed graham crackers, finely chopped peanuts, low-fat granola, about 1/2 cup of each, optional

Directions

1. Combine the dates, water, and lemon juice in a medium saucepan. Simmer over medium heat breaking up any large pieces of dates with a spoon, until the mixture resembles a thick paste, 15 to 20 minutes. Stir in the honey, peanut butter, cocoa powder, butter and salt until evenly combined. Stir in the graham crackers and oats. Remove from heat.

2. Lightly mist a baking sheet with cooking spray. Drop level tablespoons of the cookie mixture onto the prepared pan. Refrigerate until just chilled and set, about 20 minutes.

3. Put desired optional toppings in small bowls. Roll each cookie in desired topping and flatten slightly into a plump disk. Cover and refrigerate until firm. Serve chilled.

23118120R00019

Printed in Poland
by Amazon Fulfillment
Poland Sp. z o.o., Wrocław